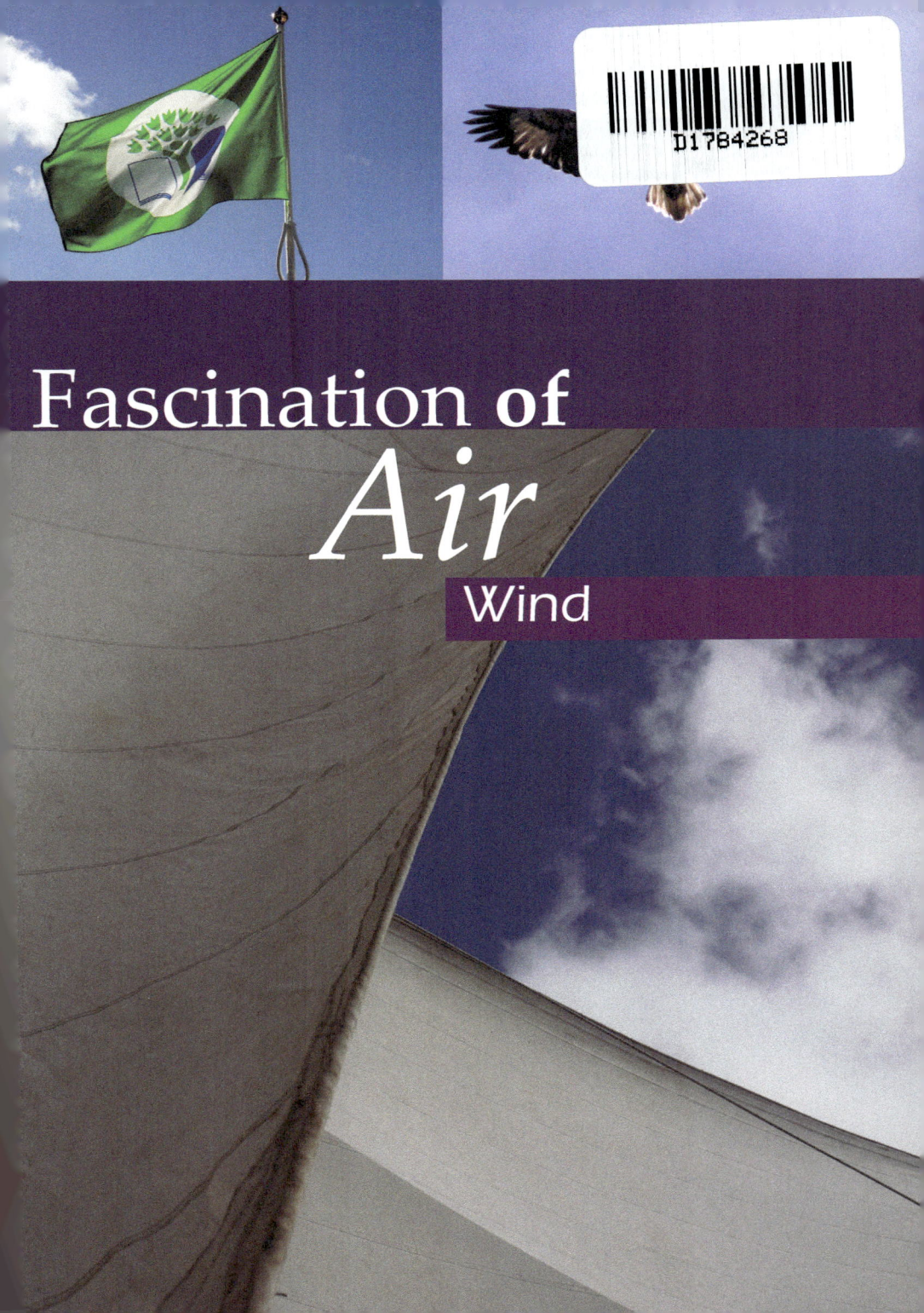

Fascination of
Air

Wind

Many thanks to Dan Phillips, Kate Hookham, Steven White and Petra Babikova, for their contribution and in making this book possible.

Special thanks go to all the children for whom we are in contact with on a daily basis for their joy and inspiration.

The rights of Claire Warden to be identified as the author of this work have been asserted in accordance with the Copyright Designs and Patents Act 1988

Design and layout by Almond www.almondtds.com +44 (0)131 553 5523

Printed by Bell & Bain, Glasgow, UK

Photography by Claire Warden and the Kindergarten teams.

All photographs © Mindstretchers Ltd 2013

ISBN 978-1-906116-14-9

For further information about Mindstretchers publications and the full range of learning resources, email enquiries@mindstretchers.co.uk

Mindstretchers™
The Old School
Fowlis Wester
Crieff
PH7 3NL
Scotland, UK
T: +44 (0)1764 650030
E: enquiries@mindstretchers.co.uk
W: www.mindstretchers.co.uk

Foreword

by Stuart Brooks

Chief Executive of the John Muir Trust

"THE mountain winds, like the dew and rain, sunshine and snow, are measured and bestowed with love on the forests to develop their strength and beauty. However restricted the scope of other forest influences, that of the winds is universal. The snow bends and trims the upper forests every winter, the lightning strikes a single tree here and there, while avalanches mow down thousands at a swoop as a gardener trims out a bed of flowers. But the winds go to every tree, fingering every leaf and branch and furrowed bole; not one is forgotten; the Mountain Pine towering with outstretched arms on the rugged buttresses of the icy peaks, the lowliest and most retiring tenant of the dells; they seek and find them all, caressing them tenderly, bending them in lusty exercise, stimulating their growth, plucking off a leaf or limb as required, or removing an entire tree or grove, now whispering and cooing through the branches like a sleepy child, now roaring like the ocean; the winds blessing the forests, the forests the winds, with ineffable beauty and harmony as the sure result." Extract from, The Mountains of California, 1894 by John Muir.

This quote from John Muir, a founding father of the modern conservation movement, sets the scene for one of his most notorious adventures. To experience the power of the wind, its relationship with nature and just to get a better view he climbed a 100ft Douglas Spruce tree during a winter storm in 1874. It was quite a ride – but the wind made it distinct, how it raked the hillsides and carried their scent, the cacophony of sound created in the remote wilderness.

John Muir experienced nature first hand and in this book Claire Warden encourages us to do just that. With so many dimensions to this most ephemeral of the elements there is an expansive range of curricular links to follow. But the book also encourages us to explore, to play and to learn with nature not just about it. I'm sure John Muir would have approved.

Contents

The movement of air around the globe controls so many facets of our being. We are often only aware of the wind when it is announced by a pilot on a plane as being responsible for the speed of a journey; or when we look up at the sky to see the clouds move above us; or for most of us at ground level, as we feel it actually touch our faces, or move our hair.

The air around us is taken for granted and yet, as a natural element, we should be seeking to protect it above all other elements, as it is so vital to our being. We can see pollution sitting as a visible band over the main cities of the world and yet, when we look at the place of studying air in the curriculum, it is often limited to making adult-designed kites or designing weather stations.

This book of fascination is designed to show the learning pathway between the multiple environments of inside, outside and 'beyond', with children from 2 to 11 years old. Fascination of Air – Wind, offers educators the chance to examine the learning beyond the obvious; to listen to children's voices as they share with us their fascinations about the wind they feel and watch, as it moves the world around them.

C. Warden.

Claire Warden 2013

Chapter 1. What is wind?

Wind is a wonderful, invisible force that affects all facets of our lives, from effective drying on a mundane washing day, to travel in hot air balloons, to global climate systems. Wind can change our mood and it moves across all parts of the face of our plane.

It is of no surprise then that children find it fascinating:

- How can the air be invisible and yet so essential?
- How does it vary its strength from a gentle wisp to a destructive force?
- How does it know what direction to move in?
- How does it manage to use its strength to erode the hard rocks and landscape?
- How does it change how cold it feels?

The fascination with the wind and deeper conversations with children has pushed the adults working with them. They may have to cast their minds back to long-forgotten geography lessons, to consider the knowledge that they have in order to create intentional moments with children that address some of their wondering questions.

How is wind created?

Wind is the movement of air. It is created when air moves from an area of high pressure to an area of low pressure. Since pressure systems vary across the surface of the earth, we have air moving around the earth constantly. Where the wind meets the bumpy surface of the earth the force of friction slows it down.

The wind can be moving at different levels and at different speeds within the atmosphere and so we can lie in the stillness of a meadow and look up at clouds moving across the sky. Atmospheric air movement is also affected by the different temperatures at the equator and the poles, which in turn, are affected by the earth's rotation on its axis.

Some of the windiest places in Scotland, are the Orkney and Shetland Islands, with winds being recorded at Force 12 using the Beaufort Scale (Sir Francis Beaufort, 1805), and potentially causing a lot of damage. The greater the wind speed, the greater the damage. Most damaging winds are commonly known as hurricanes or tornadoes.

When the sun shines down on the planet, the air closest to the ground will get warmer. Warm air rises and cooler air moves underneath it, creating wind as it moves across the landscape. The faster the air moves, the stronger the wind blows. The children of Auchlone Nature Kindergarten, Scotland, often question its existence, as not seeing it, can encourage a sense of disbelief for children. How do we begin to teach winds existence? The first thing we do is to feel and sense the wind, and watch its effect on ourselves and our environment; we discuss what we know about wind and share our knowledge on this (*see chapter 2*).

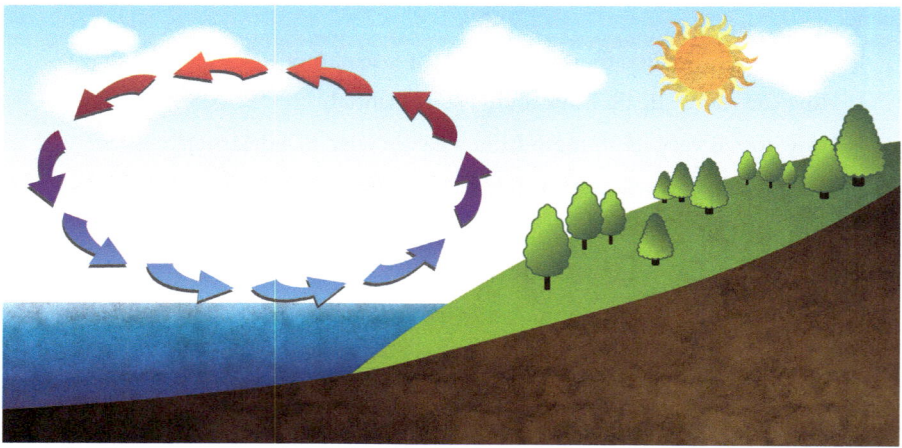

Wind formation: Day

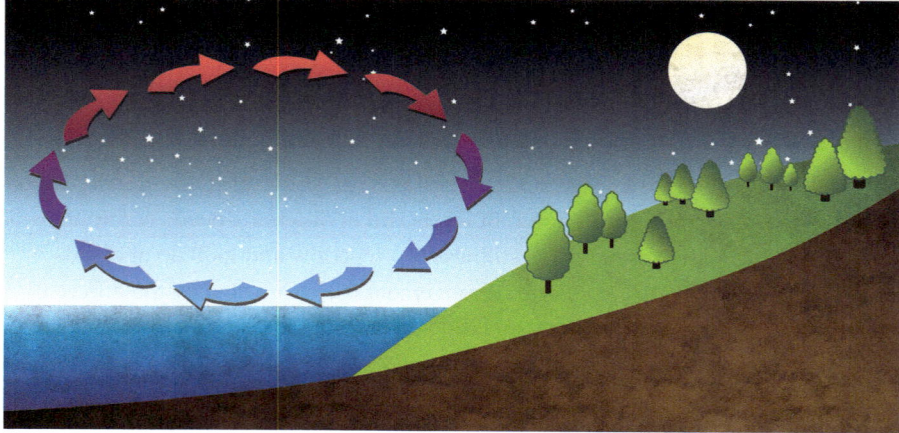

Wind formation: Night

'The universe tells you everything you need to know about it, as long as you are prepared to watch, listen, smell, in short to observe…' (Howtoons, 2006)

There are different temperatures during the day and night, that heat up or cool the land. The earth absorbs the heat of the sun and stores it. The land gives out some of the heat and warms up the air above it. The warm air rises, leaving a space for the colder, heavier air to be drawn into it. This is called a convection current.

In coastal areas, the solid earth and the liquid water heat up at different rates. The sea breeze moves in land as the land warms the air faster during the day. At night, the liquid water still has some warmth and slowly releases it, warming the air above the sea. At this point, the sea breeze changes direction and the wind blows from the heavier cold air above the land to the warmer sea.

Thermals

A thermal is a column of rising hot air. As it rises, it cools and starts to move back down to earth. The land surface can create thermals, as the surface creates smaller protected spaces that prevent the air from dispersing. Watching the birds move up and down thermals, is the easiest way to see an invisible movement of air. Humans, use the thermals when they use any form of glider, from hang glider to paraglider.

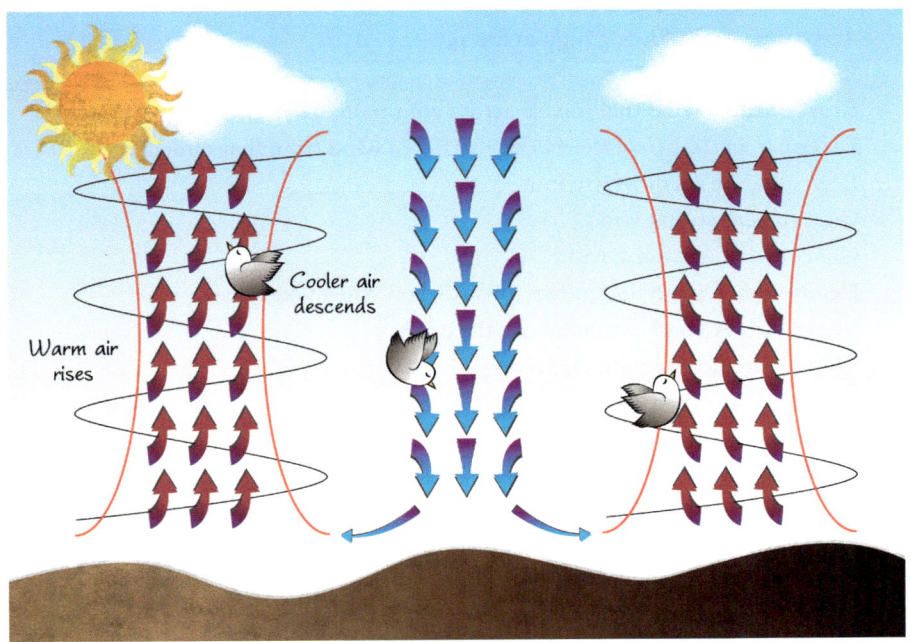

Cooler air descends

Warm air rises

Air columns formed by convection air currents

Fascinations over the years

Many cultures around the world have used stories and characters to explain the behaviours of nature. Sometimes, the stories and characters create the basis of religion. There are an endless variety to explore with children, here are a few to explore for their traditional tales.

> Vayu is the Hindu god of wind; Venti are the Roman gods of the winds; The Greeks believed that the winds were in fact gods, this god was known as Anemoi, and assigned each direction its own name; Fjin, is the Japanese wind god, and is one of the eldest Shinto gods – according to legend, he was present at the creation of the world and first let the winds out of his bag to clear the world of mist; in Norse mythology, Njord is the god of the wind.

The unseen power of the wind is often given personality and characteristics that have become words that are integrated into the language of the culture, or of the land. Some words stem from historic or cultural developments in language, such as a reliance on the wind for travel, or as the bringer of migratory birds and animals. Words are wonderful to explore with children, I particularly like the mental imagery of a dust devil!

Here are some examples:

Airstream - one blowing high in the sky

Breeze - a light wind

Crosswind - a wind that travels across your path

Easterly / westerly, southerly / northerly - a wind from that direction

Dust devil - a small whirlwind

Gale - a very strong wind

Gust - a sudden strong wind

Headwind - a wind that moves towards you when you travel

Jet stream - A wind current above the earth

Mistral - a cold dry wind in France

Prevailing wind - a wind that blows in that way at set times of the year

Sea breeze - a wind that blows on/off the shoreline

Sirocco - a hot wind that often brings dust and begins in the Sahara

Tailwind - a wind that blows you in the direction you are travelling

Tornado / 'twister'- a wind that moves in a spiral very quickly

Turbulence - unsettled wind

Whirlwind - wind that spins very, very quickly

Zephyr - a gentle wind

Measuring the wind

The need to look at wind patterns and strengths was key to understanding how to keep safe. Now there is enough technology available to look at the patterns, flows, pressure systems from satellites.

In 1805, British Admiral, Sir Francis Beaufort, made a scale in order to easily describe the speed of winds at sea. It is called the Beaufort Scale. To date, the Beaufort Scale remains in use and still stands as a great guidance for sea goers, being used in the shipping forecasts in the UK. Warnings range from 'small craft warning', if winds of Beaufort force 6 (mean wind speed exceeding 22 knots) are expected up to 10 nautical miles offshore, to 'Hurricane Force Warnings' if winds of greater than 64 knots are expected.

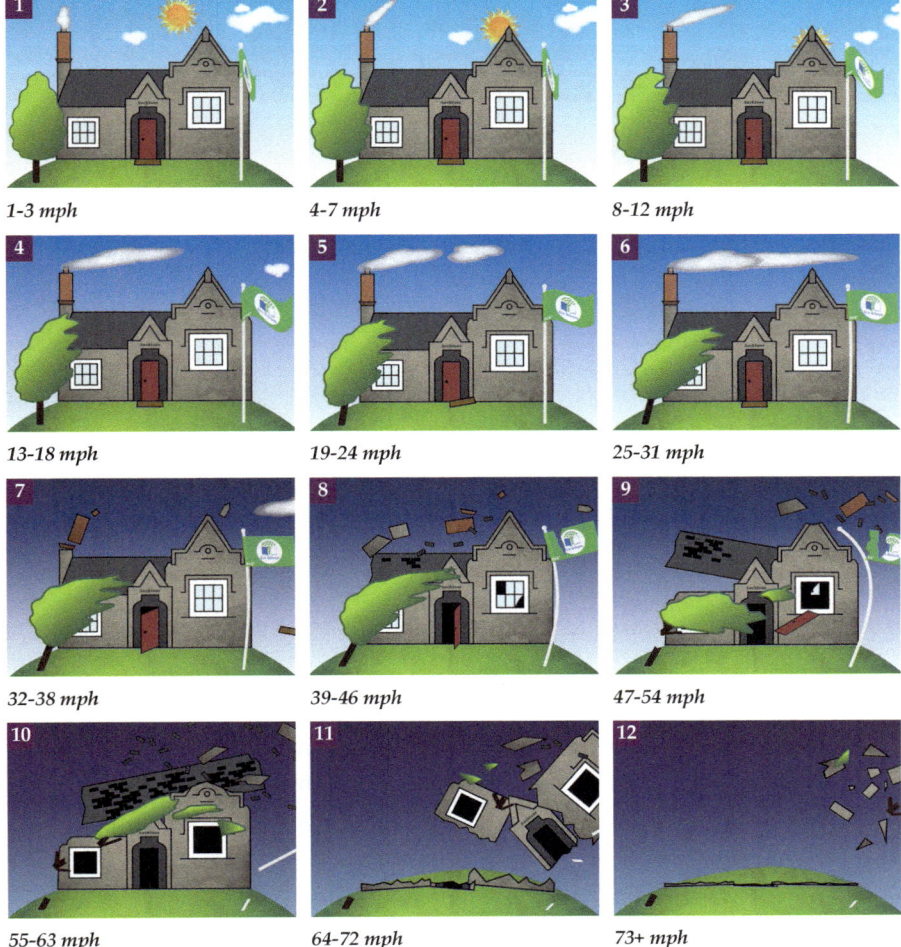

1-3 mph	4-7 mph	8-12 mph
13-18 mph	19-24 mph	25-31 mph
32-38 mph	39-46 mph	47-54 mph
55-63 mph	64-72 mph	73+ mph

Harnessing the wind

Transportation

Sailing ships use the wind for propulsion. The wind is 'caught' in a variety of sail types and positions on the boat that enables sailors to harness the wind, irrespective of the wind direction. Each sail has a different name, and boats have a different number of sails on a variety of number of masts. For example, pinnakers are very large curved sails at the front of the boat that are designed to catch even the lightest of breezes.

For aerodynamic aircraft, the direction of wind and its velocity affect its direction for takeoff and landing. Many airports have many runways, in a variety of directions, so that the aircraft can be sent to use the most appropriate in relation to its direction.

Recreation

The desire to move, has created a wide range of hobbies and sports linked to the wind.

The Montgolfier brothers, born in Annonay, France, were the inventors of the first practical balloon, although highly ornate and only affordable by the rich. The first demonstrated flight of a hot air balloon took place on June 4, 1783, in Annonay, France. Their balloon lifted 6,562 feet off the ground.

Wind figures prominently in several popular sports which are now accessible to many people through clubs, including recreational hang gliding, hot air ballooning, kite flying, snow kiting, kite land boarding, kite surfing, paragliding, sailing, and windsurfing.

The power of the wind

Effect on plants

Wind dispersal of seeds is one of the more primitive means of dispersal. There are two ways that nature has used the wind to distribute seeds. The two most common forms are through:

a) The blowing of a seed that has a parachute or feathery systems, so that the seed is lifted up and floats away on the breeze e.g. dandelion, rose bay willow herb, thistledown.

b) The dropping of seeds from taller plants, such as trees with wings to enable the distribution away from the main plant e.g. sycamore seeds.

Wind dispersal is a very random method of distribution, in that the seeds can land anywhere. In order to overcome this, the plants have to produce very large numbers of seed to ensure that the seed lands on fertile land.

Wind can affect the growth of plants. Trees demonstrate stunted and misshapen

growth over many years of prevailing winds, training the plants to grow into the area of least resistance. The wind also exposes roots on the windward side, and the trees can seem to have all their roots above ground. However, the plant has adapted by growing down, away from the wind into the area where there is often more soil as it is sheltered from erosion.

Effect on animals

The wind chill factor cools any animal, from humans to sheep and cows. Many animals who live outside, turn their backs to the prevailing wind to minimise the area of their bodies exposed to the wind, and to reduce the effect of wind chill. Or conversely, use the wind to cool them down or dry them off, by understanding wind direction. Smaller animals, such as insects, use the wind for transportation, landing wherever the wind takes them to.

Harnessing wind has become a sport and a sustainable energy source for hundreds of years. The simple process of flying a kite, or watching a seed turn, has now inspired people to create commercial endeavours that rely on the wind. Wind powered pumps drained the polders of the Netherlands, and in arid regions, such as the American mid-west or the Australian outback, wind pumps provided water for live stock and steam engines. There are records that suggest that some of the people in 300BC, used their knowledge of the wind to create furnaces from monsoon winds that reached 2,190°F (1,200°F). Windmills were used in Afghanistan in the 7th century, to pump water for irrigation, and now technology is being developed to explore high altitude wind capture.

The desire for electricity led people to look at wind turbines to generate power. The wind turbines vary in size to provide energy for remote dwellings through to villages, and now, as a form of renewable energy that feeds into the national power grid in some countries such as the UK.

In the arts

The wind is ephemeral, and its transience and movement have captured artists imaginations for generations. The desire to capture that elusive moment has driven artists to investigate the movement of nature in the form of leaves, grass, clouds, trees, and birds.

Claude Monet, in his painting 'Poplars in Wind' (1891), is an example where the observer can distinguish the winds effect on the poplars as it is captured in time.

Van Gogh, depicts wind through his paintings, for example with a flying bird and windswept clouds to depict their movement in space and time.

The human power to blow, in essence to create wind, has had a long lasting effect on the purpose and style of musical instruments. The use of music can capture the profound effect that wind has on our being. Most folk music for winds imitates vocal models, such as the folk music for the harmonica played often in the USA, along with the flute - love songs played by Native American men, and no one can mistake the distinctive sound of the bagpipes – the music of Scotland. Many countries across Europe, use variations of wind instruments to tell their folk story through music.

Songs that are about the wind speak of change, such as Bob Dylan's song; 'Blowing in the Wind'. Wind in lyrics is often used as a metaphor to describe strong and powerful emotions and feelings, for example, The Beatles; 'The long and Winding Road', that includes the lyrics: '... the wild and windy nights', suggests emotions in turmoil.

The composition of music often mimics the wind as it rises and falls, howls, whistles and blasts through the air. This poetic element is present in all genres of music, from Wagner to Brahms, Stravinsky, Debussy, Schubert, Charlie Parker, Duke Ellington, Count Basie and Miles Davis to name but a few.

Poems by adults, have been written to stimulate their fascination with wind, our connection and use of it, to why we question its existence and its effect on us and the environment. Poems demonstrate this wonderfully, such as Christina Rossetti's; 'Who Has Seen the Wind?' that express the wind's invisibility and movement, as does a poem by Leslie Tryon simply called 'Wind'.

'Untitled' by Emily Warden

'Wind' by Emily Warden

'Tornado' by Emily Warden

Chapter 2. Case Studies with Analysis and Possible Lines of Development

Case study 1: Creating kites

It was a sunny but breezy summers day at Auchlone Camp. The children decided it was the perfect day to fly a kite. Unfortunately, we did not have any available, and so the children decided to design and make them.

An older boy said: "We need light materials, if they are heavy it just won't take off. Kate, what have we got?"

Kate (practitioner), went off to see what she could find, she brought a range of materials consisting of sticks, balsa wood, straws, cane, plastic bags, tissue paper, cardboard and plain paper.

"This paper is the lightest and brightest."

One of the girls said. "We should use this stuff." The children then put aside the plastic bags, cardboard and plain paper leaving just the tissue paper.

Next, the frame. They placed the different materials (sticks, balsa and straws) in each hand and then lifted the items up and down to compare weights to try to find the lightest. They decided after much swapping. "Because we don't have 3 hands!" said a 3 year old, that balsa wood was sturdy, light and would be the best material for the frame.

Finally, to the design, the children recalled kites they had had in the past:

"I had a diamond shaped one with a long tail," said a girl.

"I have a square one," said a three year old.

"I've got one that goes all the way round with a hole in it." said another 3 year old.

"My dad has one that lifts him off the ground and is really, really, really big!" said an older boy.

"Yeah, my dad knows someone that get's pulled along on a buggy up at St Andrew's beach," said another older boy.

"Wow, how big would we need to make one to pull us up in the air?" said the first older boy.

"I'm gonna make a stunt kite," comments the eldest boy.

Kate offers, "Well, in Indonesia, they make a lot of stunt kites and they are the diamond shape you talked about, like two triangles joined together. Triangles are a very strong shape!"

"Yes, it would be hard to do a circle, but we could use dogwood or willow," said the eldest boy.

"You can try that," commented Kate.

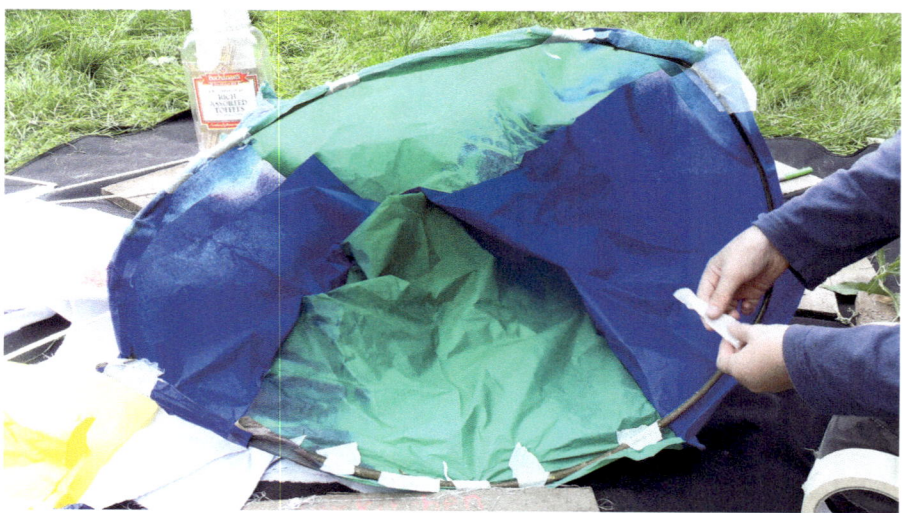

"Lets try different ones," said the girl.

The children then created their own kites using the tissue paper, balsa wood and their own designs and shapes (some diamond, some square, some 'TIE-fighter' from Star Wars) … we even had one with a window!

We then left the kites to dry over lunchtime. "So they are as light as possible," said the older boy again.

After lunch, we had to make our final decision. How long should our line be?

Unfortunately, by this point and being Scotland, the weather had changed and the wind had dropped! The children were not discouraged. They tried using long strings, but the kites just dragged along the ground. "Because there is not enough wind." said the older boy, "We could just make them short lines and run really fast." This is what they did and we had success running up and down the garden.

After a few goes, one of the girls said, " Hold on, we are going to bump into one another … we need to make a runway – lets do it out on the track." The whole group of 3-13 year olds, then moved out onto the forest track and ran outbound, away from the garden with kites trailing in the air – just! When the children ran out of breath, they stopped and walked along the edge of the track homebound, back to the start.

Analysis of learning

This learning experience started with nature, the strong breeze led the children to want to explore the wind's power by creating kites. In creating their own kites, they explored the properties of a range of materials for the frame and 'sail'. This experimentation lead to a scientific exploration of the properties of these materials; which are strong? Which break easily? What can be used to combine these elements? This was extended into mathematical thinking, looking at the weight of these materials and the strength of different shapes.

Art and design also played a role in this learning story. Children selected one or several colours and chose a shape of their choice, even making 'windows' and decorated their 'tails'.

When flying the kites, the children self- risk assessed, deciding that running all over the garden may lead to a collision. Therefore, a one way 'runway' was set up with children walking carefully back down the side of the 'runway'. This resulted in the children being able to pick up greater speed, without fear of collision with others.

PLODS

1) Investigate futher the properties of tissue paper, and how this can be used to make stronger materials i.e. papier mache with PVA glue. Would a stronger but heavier material be better for a kite?

2) Bring in a range of real kites, or take photographs from the internet to look at their design compared to our designs. What are the similarities and the differences? What effect does shape have on a kite?

3) Explore runways at airports and how safety is managed on a large scale to avoid collision in the air and on the ground.

Case study 2:
Harnessing the winds energy: windmills

A succession of very windy days led to a discussion about windmills and the power of the wind. The children discussed how they could make their own windmills to test the strength of the wind outside. Maia suggested using 'a little, tiny stick and leaves' to make her windmill and Struan and Rosa decided they wanted to use 'leaves and sticks' too. Isla thought we 'could use paper for the front and we could use something sharp to cut a hole' so that we could place it on the stick.

After a few more suggestions Otto (aged 4) said:

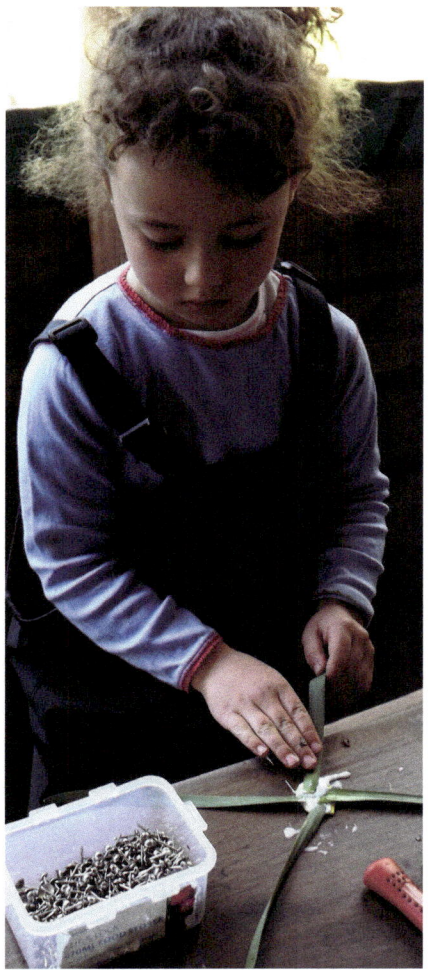

"You could make it with paper. We need to stick it on and then it would blow quite easily because paper's really light."

This started a very interesting discussion regarding the weight of the resources to be used. "You could use leaves and a really thin stick because leaves are light." *Harrison (aged 4).* The children were asked why it was important that what they used was light and Isla answered, "It needs to be light so it will go round. It won't spin if it's heavy, all the things will just go down." Otto added, "It won't turn because everything's heavy like big stones."

The discussion continued later in the day, when the children decided to make their own windmills using a variety of different resources they had collected from both indoors and outside.

"I'm going to make mine out of green leaves." Molly (aged 3)

21

"I'm going to have some wood and one wood for the windmill then glue to put them on." Struan (aged 4)

Harrison extended his original idea from earlier; "I want to use green leaves and a nail and a hammer."

Having started on their projects, Molly decided to make it more fun, "We could have a race with them."

"Yes, we could do who makes the best." *(Harrison)*

"Or, which one turns the most times." *Iona (aged 4)*

Struan uses glue to stick different lengths of tissue paper onto his stick. Harrison uses tissue paper and pine cones which he attaches to his stick with some wire. He adds leaves to the ends of the wire and is ready to test his windmill. They both go outside to test their designs.

"Mine's spinning! Mine's spinning around!" *(Harrison)*

Struan's does not move, "I'm going to put mine somewhere else." They place their windmills in a variety of different places outside, and test out which place is the best for their windmill to work.

Inside, Molly and Iona are still working on their designs. Molly is using some glue to stick tissue paper to her stick.

"I might need some more on top.
The paper isn't sticking."

"The glue will make it hard to turn around. I need to use a nail."

Iona has collected some daffodil leaves from outside and has stuck them at 90 degree angles to a circle of foam.

"I need to leave mine to dry and then I can hammer it into a stick with the nail." (Iona)

Iona starts to make another one whilst her first dries. She uses shapes of foam that she has cut out and tapes them to a stick she has collected from outside.

"It doesn't turn because it's stuck on." *(Iona)*

She takes the tape off and uses a nail instead. She goes outside to test what she has made, but the windmill doesn't turn in the wind, even when she blows it herself.

The children reflect on the session and discuss what happened with their windmills.

"My windmill worked and it never stopped going round, it just kept on doing it and Struan's wasn't a windmill it was a flag." *(Harrison)*

"Mine was going round in circles. It didn't stop even a bit." *(Struan)*

"It did stop." *(Harrison)*

"Well, sometimes." *(Struan)*

"I think mine didn't work because it needs to be on a bigger stick. I might swop it to a bigger stick and see what happens then." *(Molly)*

"This windmill didn't work because it was stuck onto the stick with tape." *(Iona)*

"Don't use tape." *(Harrison)*

The children's discussion stops there, and they tidy up the area before going outside to experiment more with their designs.

Analysis of learning

The children were fascinated by the strength of the wind over several days and wished to explore the power of the wind and how they could 'catch it!' During a 'Talk-Around' time. We explored a mini-wind turbine from the 'Power' Talking Tub™ (see photo case study 2 insert). Having explored this 'product', the children decided they could create their own 'wind turbines' from resources found in the Nature Kindergarten.

This discussion led to an interest in the technology and the construction of windmills and wind turbines. Initial tests and discussions were linked to materials and the properties of those materials; paper, tissue paper, sticks, leaves, stones, wood, cones and wire were explored. Strength verses weight were evaluated and tested. Each child then selected their own combination of materials to create a windmill.

The second learning experience focused upon the technology which allowed their creations to rotate. Some of the children used their previous experiences of using art materials, assuming glue and paper would rotate and move. Other children built upon their Forest School and Bushcraft skills using nails and wire to ensure their 'blades' rotated. The successes and failures of these approaches were then analysed, and their creations amended appropriately to ensure each child's success criteria was met. For some children, the artistic merits of 'looking nice', outweighed the requirement to rotate and capture the wind.

On completing their own windmills, the group explored how they would create a game linked to the windmills and designed rules to determine who would be the winner. The social skills of negotiation and compromise were required to create rules that everyone agreed upon. A range of games were then played by different groups of children.

A final learning point was led by Struan, who noticed that where the windmill was sited, often effected how much it rotated. The children spent time finding the windiest parts of Auchlone using their windmills.

PLODS

1) Explore other objects that rotate and how these mechanisms work. For example, wheels on bicycles and toy cars. Children could deconstruct and reconstruct these mechanisms to explore their workings.

2) Discuss well known games and the rules associated with these games. Why do we need rules for games? If we were creating a further game or adapting an existing game, what rules would we make?

3) Explore how we measure wind (Beaufort Scale – *case study 3*) and why windmills are located where they are. Find a permanent site to measure wind (either flag or windmill, or set up a weather station).

Case study 3: Measuring the strength of the wind: Beaufort Scale

How can we measure the wind?

As it had been very windy over the past few days, the children discussed the effect the wind had on them as they arrived to the setting. Throughout the day, the children observed its impact on the forest, reflecting on the 'weather floorbook', on days where the children had created their windmills. The children discussed how strong the wind might get and what kind of damage it might create in our forest.

The question was asked by an adult:

"Do you think we can measure the wind?"

"You feel it." *Otto (aged 5)*

"It feels cold, on your arms and hands." *Harrison (aged 5)*

"Yeah, my hands get cold in the wind." *Chloe (aged 3)*

"Trees are really thick, stuck in the ground. The wind blows all leaves off." *Harrison (aged 5)*

"It's so windy, the wind blows the branches off." *Leo (aged 3)*

"You can make a windmill, like we did to measure wind; it's so strong the wind. Made our windmill so strong, make it like a tree windmill. Press a button on the tree." *Fin (aged 3)*

"If you touch the big windmills (wind-farm), it will electrocute you!" *Otto (aged 5)*

"Round and round and round. It's so strong. Won't go round if too light wind. It blows the wind; branches will fall, falls on your head and you go to the doctors. It might break Auchlone." *Fin (aged 3)*

"A thunderstorm wind will blow a tree down!" *Struan (aged 5)*

"Use something that's in the direction of the wind. Use something to show the way the wind is blowing." *Cairn (aged 5)*

"Grass will show us which direction the wind is blowing, if we pick up the grass and see." *Alick (aged 4)*

"If it was a very, very strong wind, grass would blow all the way to Germany!" *Otto (aged 5)*

"Wood is heavy so would blow away. Little sticks are light; they would blow all the way to China!" *Harrison (aged 5)*

"If there is no wind, grass will fall to the ground!" *Otto (aged 5)*

"Light wind, it will blow a little and then fall down." *Cairn (aged 5)*

"I don't think trees will fall down in a light wind, just grass." *Leo (aged 3)*

"Yeah, the trees are heavy; the wind is light, when the wind is as heavy as a tree, that's when the tree will blow down." *Cairn (aged 5)*

"It's a dark wind when trees fall over! You have a light wind and a dark wind and a strong wind!" *Lilly (aged 3)*

"A strong wind will blow feathers about!" *Fi (aged 3)*

Gathering themselves together, the children prepared for a windy day outdoors. They setup their own version of the Beaufort Scale, testing out some of the natural materials that they discussed during their 'talking and thinking' gathering.

"Here is the grass; it's staying still on my hand just now, cause there is no wind to blow it away!" Harvey (aged 4)

"If no wind is a zero, and lots of wind is a three, what number is the wind just now?" *Steve (teacher)*

"It is a big fat zero; there is no wind so it's a zero!" *Harvey (aged 4)* and dropping the grass to the floor:

"If it is a three, there will be no grass and you will have no hand left!" *Guy (aged 3)*

"I think three winds would blow sticks away! I think three winds would make the flag go out like straight, like a post!" Millie (aged 3)

"The wind makes the flag go flat when it's not there, then up a bit, and a bit more, then out like a post." Millie (aged 3)

Analysis of learning

Following a reflection upon the 'Weather floorbook' and the work undertaken in creating windmills, the children discussed how the wind affects them and the natural environment. This discussion progressed to explore how we know which direction the wind is coming from.

Children used familiar 'props' to discuss wind levels – the grass, sticks and our Eco flag. The children chose their own numerical scale of 0-3. Therefore, zero represented no wind and 3 a very strong wind. These numbers were then tagged to the behaviour of the grass, sticks and Eco flag in the breeze.

Learning outdoors is a daily occurrence at Auchlone Nature Kindergarten. Children become used to selecting the appropriate clothing for the weather conditions that day. During the initial discussions, it was mentioned that the wind feels cold. The children therefore, wear extra wind-proof items on windy days and are aware that they should monitor wind levels in the wood, to risk assess the impact upon the mature trees. Staff and children will return to the safe garden environment on days with high winds, as dead wood could be blown out of the mature trees on these days.

PLODS

1) Set up a weather station to monitor the direction and nature of the wind over a longer period of time. Do certain types of weather and wind approach from the same direction? This could be recorded in a Floorbook™ about weather.

2) Explore scales, where do we have other scales to measure (links to water gauges, weighing scales). The actual Beaufort Scale could be shared with the children and compared to the scale they have created.

3) Children should conduct further risk assessments with staff to explore different weather conditions, and their affect on humans and the natural environment.

Area of enquiry

1. Knowledge about the creation of wind (Case study 3)
2. Observations of wind (Case study 3)
3. Experimentation with the wind (Case study 1 & 2)

Area of enquiry

1. Wind as a provocation for artistic expression (Case study 1 & 2)
2. Wind as a resource for creativity (Case study 1 & 2)

Area of enquiry

1. Development of technology in windmill design (Case study 2)
2. Technology as a method of collecting evidence (Case study 2)

Area of enquiry

1. Recording mathematical thinking (Case study 3)
2. Mathematical concepts (Case study 1)

Area of enquiry

1. Wind as a stimulation for different types of writing
2. Speaking and listening on a day when the wind is noticeable because it is strong or absent
3. Narrative linked to the wind
4. Functional talk (Case study 3)

Area of enquiry

1. Children's awareness and management of risk (Case study 1)
2. Active outdoor learning experiences (Case study 1, 2 & 3)
3. Wind is needed to make our weather and climate work
4. The earth is a system that needs the movement of air

Area of enquiry

1. Historical use of wind by humans (Case study 2)
2. Natural resources in the environment (Case study 3)
3. Weather: wind and its effects on the environment
4. Exuberance and joy

Area of enquiry concept/knowledge/skill	Opportunities for experiential learning experiences
1. Knowledge about the creation of wind	
Wind is created when there are two areas of pressure. High and low. These cause the air to move causing wind.	This is a complex concept, as it exists at an atmospheric level. Use phrases such as: 'the wind is air moving from a place where there is no room, to a place where it has more room.' Explore making a paper aeroplane and how the aeroplane relies on varying pressure to keep it up.
We can make the air move to create wind.	Children often get confused with the idea that they create the wind when they run, as it feels as if their hair is being blown up just as it does when the wind actually blows it. To create wind, the simplest way is to wave a cardboard/fan to make the air move. Children can then stand still, see the air being moved and feel its effect.
2. Observations of wind	
Wind is a powerful force, it can lift/move objects.	The strength of the wind fascinates children. They can see leaves being moved and hear the wind in the trees. When a major event of some force happens, it can alter their understandings and feel very strange and unsettling. When a tree fell down in the storms, the children were obviously affected. Dialogue and observations allowed children to work through many things, one of which was the power of the wind.
Wind moves objects in different ways.	Create opportunities to watch the wind as it lifts the dry leaves or the sand/dry dirt; lie down to watch the top of the trees move, or the clouds move across the sky. In sandy/dry environments, explore the wind created environments (Aeolian). Explore the effects of wind upon water surfaces. Look for eddies and vortices in corners where the shape of the building often causes the wind to rotate, spinning the smaller objects around.

Area of enquiry concept/knowledge/skill	Opportunities for experiential learning experiences
3. Experimentation with the wind	
Moving air is measured to give a number to its strength (Beaufort Scale).	Allow children to experiment with different materials to investigate the way that the wind can be measured, e.g. the way it moves hair, moves leaves, a windmill, a ribbon, the plants, the tops of the trees.
	The creation of own wind-rating scales, with choice of numbers and indicators of strength.
Wings help objects move in the wind.	Exploration and investigation of the purpose of wings; from 'glitzy' wings for the children, to natural 'wings' on seed cases (e.g. sycamore) and feathers to manmade wings, planes and windmills.
Kites fly in the wind due to their shape and mass.	Kite design should involve a wide range of possibilities and experimentation. For young children, a plastic bag tied to a string is a kite, as they develop an awareness of other possibilities, they can explore making them from willow and tissue paper. Kite making can seem childlike and yet it involves very complex aerodynamics and can therefore, be fraught with frustrations when the kite struggles to work.
Windmills come in all shapes and sizes.	The Talking Tub™ allows the adult to offer pictures and models to widen the breadth of awareness of the children, before they start to explore ways of making objects turn.
	For young children, the pivot and its movement are the key, and could be provided by the adult in the form of bicycle wheels or frameworks that can then be added to create unique windmills.

Area of enquiry concept/knowledge/skill	Opportunities for experiential learning experiences
1. Wind as a provocation for artistic expression	
Wind makes sounds when it moves itself and objects.	Stop and listen to the wind as it gently moves the trees, or whips up the waves. The rustling of leaves, or the wind whistling through a tiny gap can be extended into larger experiences to record soundscapes. Record these sounds.
Wind can make us feel like moving.	The wind has an effect on children. Usually, very calm children become excitable by it, as it moves us and plays with us so we feel playful in our hearts. Dancing and moving in an exuberant way with the wind can all happen wherever you are outside. Drawing, in response to the wind, can give wonderful visual collages.

Area of enquiry concept/knowledge/skill	Opportunities for experiential learning experiences
2. Wind as a resource for creativity	
Wind changes the shapes around us.	The effect of wind on a field of long grass or a wheat crop, creates a constantly moving textural and colourful montage that can fascinate and engage children when they have time to watch it.
	Trees grow in relation to the wind direction on the outer islands in Scotland. They are often short and grow in the leeward direction, creating unusual shapes.
	Aolian (wind created) landscapes, in rock based spaces are often stunningly beautiful and fascinating to children. The small ridges and hollows offer dips and shapes to explore for making mud soup and hiding spaces for tiny folk. We can deepen and widen this fascination by offering larger Aolian landscapes in the photos in the Talking Tub™. For example, sand dunes in the Sahara, mountain spaces such as in Utah, USA . Each of these may stimulate Lines of Enquiry in the sand area, as the new awareness is integrated into the play.
Wind can move water.	Observe and photograph any water form; the movement patterns on the surface of a puddle to the ripple effect on the sea/lake and notice as the wind whips the spray from the top of a wave.
Wind can move mobiles we create.	Design of natural dream catchers or wind mobiles, using nature's treasures of feathers, seed pods and sticks. The mobiles should be hung up outside rather than inside, so that children can see the way the different weights move (mass and velocity).
Wind can affect our mood and emotions.	Look at poems and rhymes that explore the wind in a little more detail. Young children should be exposed to poetry that seems complex, as the tone of the adult voice reading and the intonation and patterning of the voice, has an effect on their long term love of poetry.

Area of enquiry concept/knowledge/skill	Opportunities for experiential learning experiences
1. Development of technology in windmill design	
Air can be harnessed in many ways.	The creation of windmills leads children into the world of wind turbines and their presence in the landscape. They are surrounded by controversy in Scotland and elsewhere in the world, so the age of the children should dictate how involved the discussion becomes. Always give a balanced picture.
2. Technology as a method of collecting evidence	
Wind can be collected and measured.	Setting up a weather station, is more appropriate to older children who feel they wish to follow statistical surveys. With younger children, the creative process of design and problem solving is a key part of their fascination. Noticing and engaging are important aspects of all ages.

Area of enquiry concept/knowledge/skill	Opportunities for experiential learning experiences
1. Recording mathematical thinking	
Information handling and recording using charts, pictograms and tallies, help us to see trends or change in wind and weather conditions.	The use of child created windmills gives children a provocation for mathematical thinking. Creation of tables, tallymarks, awareness of the possibilities of how to record velocity.
2. Mathematical concepts	
Angle and shape affect how streamline an objects and the impact of wind upon it.	Shape and pattern linked to the design of objects that use the wind to move, i.e. seed flight. Look at the designs in nature and why trees and animals/birds are that shape and form. Recreate shape and hold objects at different angles to explore the impact of wind.
Wind strength and size are often linked, larger gusts of wind more larger objects. Wind speed affects movement in time.	Measures: explore size linked to perimeter and area (kite making); time (wind speed).Try to measure wind speed using a range of objects, you could even try to make your own anemometer.
Numbers are used to denote the power of wind on the Beaufort Scale.	Number: numeral shape and quantity used in context for the measurement of wind force. Explore the value of 1 compared to 4 on the Beaufort Scale, or even wind speed on water. Make up your own number scales exploring value/quantity of wind.

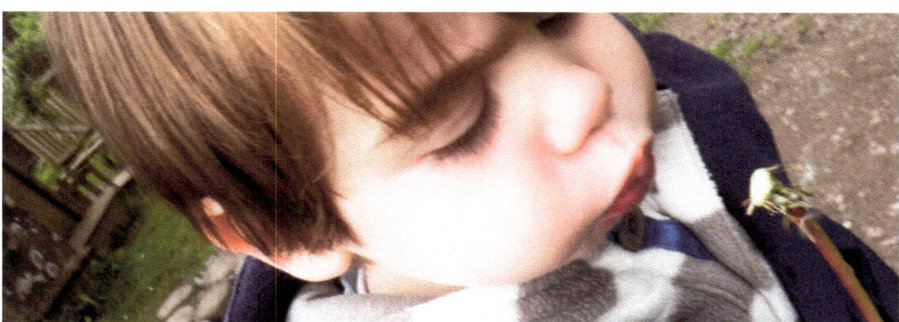

Area of enquiry concept/knowledge/skill	Opportunities for experiential learning experiences
1. Wind as a stimulation for different types of writing	
	Use wind as the stimulation to encourage children to write in a variety of genres, from functional instructions of how to make a windmill, to writing poetry to describe emotions and feelings about wind. The fact that children can do so many things with air, will mean that it is a perfect object for them to use as a focus for discussion and writing.
2. Speaking and listening on a day when the wind is noticeable because it is strong or absent	
	The experience of just being in the wind, or watching the wind push the clouds across the sky, can create a focussed atmosphere that supports children to take part in a range of speaking and listening activities.
	Enquiry questions can be linked to any area of the curriculum: where does the wind come from? How does it know what direction to blow?
	Experiment with talking into and away from the wind: how does it affect our voice and ability to hear.
3. Narrative linked to the wind	
	Stories such as 'The Blue Balloon' by Nick Inkpen.
	Storytelling with objects that have a variety of weights (mass), so that the story can explore the relationship of wind strength and weight of objects. Include a compass to provoke talk about direction.
4. Functional talk	
	Record frameworks of understanding in the Floorbook™ to share children's theories.

Literacy

Health and Well Being	Area of enquiry concept/knowledge/skill	Opportunities for experiential learning experiences
1. Children's awareness and management of risk		
	Children are able to self-risk assess, and the more we can trust them to make decisions and provide supportive environments for them to do so, the more they will thrive.	Children can be supported to create their own Benefit-Risk Assessment about being outside in the wind. This will encourage them to make decisions about how to look after themselves and others. The risk assessment can be written down by children, or recorded in their own words by an adult. On our site, an understanding of the wind's impact upon the mature trees, and our safety associated with this is vital.
2. Active outdoor learning experiences		
	Children need to be active and outdoors.	Children can be encouraged to explore the outdoor area and look for signs of strong wind. The hazards of high winds need to have an overview by the adult. Children love to run in and hide from the wind.

Area of enquiry concept/knowledge/skill	Opportunities for experiential learning experiences
1. Historical use of wind by humans	
Air is required by all people on the earth to survive.	Explore how it is used, apart from being a basic requirement, varies from one culture to another through religion, industry or recreation. Use the internet and other secondary sources to widen their awareness of the variety of life and living conditions on the Earth.
2. Natural resources in the environment	
Air quality affects people, plants and animals.	Awareness of the need for clean air will come from the prolonged access to being outside. For older children, create the Talking Tub™ to include imagery of air pollution/pollution masks etc.
Wind is needed to make our weather and climate work.	As developmentally appropriate, explore the technology to watch the movement of the clouds and wind on a global scale. Weather forecasting and media use of monitoring weather.
The earth is a system that needs the movement of air.	As developmentally appropriate, investigate migration patterns of birds, dispersal of seeds, seasonal variation. An awareness of how the seasons may, or may not change in various parts of the world, can be explored through the flow of wind currents around the world.
3. Wind and its effects on the landscape	
	Research the impact wind has on us and the environment. Investigate the impact wind has when it erodes away the landscape, and what happens when wind causes damage.
4. Exuberance and Joy	
Being out in the wind is invigorating and exciting.	The sheer joy of playing in the wind as it whips up hair and light objects should not be underestimated, laughter and demonstrations of happiness should be encouraged.

Chapter 4. Developing Skills

1. Floating soapy bubbles
(by Steven, 33 years old)

Bubbles are a tantalizing entity of awe and wonder. Not only do they float effortlessly, they sparkle with a display of colours. At Auchlone we make a variety of bubble making kits.

1. Fill a basin full of lukewarm water.
2. Finely cut a bar of soap into shavings and break up in warm water (for better results, add a few drops of glycerine).
3. Add the soapy water to the lukewarm water.
4. Immerse the tip of a drinking straw or similar (small piece of bamboo) into a basin.
5. Blow carefully, the trick is to stop blowing just before the bubbles burst, until you are happy with the bubble. Hopefully, it will soar into the sky ...

2. Windcatcher
(by Cairn, 4 years old)

There are many traditional weathervanes out there, but before you go rushing to buy one, look around in nature and your setting to create your own from the materials that you have found.

1. Put long bits of material on a tree, because you need to see them in the wind, and they catch the light wind (*any secure fitting will do e.g. post , fence, stick*).

2. Tie bits of string with pinecones on them, so when the wind is strongest, they won't fly away, and you can see the strong wind blow.

3. Weave in string and other bits (*materials, grasses, sticks and willow*) to catch the wind and keep it there.

4. You have to do all this in the windiest bit possible in the nursery.

3. Parachutes

(by Euan, 7 years old)

In Auchlone Nature Kindergarten, we have found that the children enjoy making their own small parachutes as much as they do flying one, we have created square, rectangular, triangular, hexagonal, single and double tiered parachutes of many different colours and materials, so before buying one, here are some steps that we use to make our own.

1. Get yourself some paper or cloth, I prefer paper because I can use different colours. Put leaves and sticks on the paper, and paint it with glue so the stay on.

2. You need to tie little bits of string or twine to the corners of the paper or cloth.

3. Tie the string or twine (*in the centre, as a weight*) onto a big nail, a big nail is best because it is heavy and will bring the parachute down, but not too fast!

4. You need to try different sizes of nails for it to work. If the nail is too heavy, it will drop too fast to the ground and if it is too light, it won't work either, because it will float away!

Chapter 5. Benefit-Risk Assessment

Benefit-Risk Assessment	Wind based activities
Assessment date: Aug 2012	Date for review: August 2013 - ongoing
Assessment undertaken by:	Staff member
Approved by:	Senior staff member
Local or site specific hazard considerations: (add for your site)	Unstable tree branches, low level branches. Structural damage to any buildings. Loose materials not sufficiently secured.
Benefits of activity:	• Opportunity for children to self-risk assess • Group co-operation • Group awareness • Build self-confidence • Build independence and develop trust • Develop gross and fine motor skills • Explore childrens strength • Understand the power of the wind • Understand the impact of wind upon the local environment – plants and animals • Harness the wind to power objects • Scientific exploration • Weather forecasting and understanding weather conditions • Learn how to use tools safely • Learn about the properties and uses of different materials and resources • Artistic expression

Hazard	Level of risk	Precaution	Revised risk level
Weather: e.g. wind, rain, sun, snow, hail, sleet, fog, thunder and lightening, daily temperature	Medium /High	• Monitor daily weather forecasts and amend activity/location of learning appropriately • Monitor weather conditions during session and amend activity as appropriate • Wear appropriate clothing for weather conditions • Apply sunscreen if require • Erect shelters when required • Ensure you can see/hear children at all times • Monitor the warmth and well-being of the children, amend activity as appropriate • Adults assess the impact of weather on upon local environment – tree canopy in particular	Low
Children	Low/ Medium	• Staff received training in working with vulnerable groups and are security checked • Adult ratios are appropriate to age and needs of children • Staff are aware of specific needs of each child (social, emotional, behavioural, medical, ability, knowledge) and manage/monitor this accordingly • Children are made aware of weather conditions and additional actions to take e.g. clothing, behaviour • Interaction between children is monitored and managed as appropriate	Low

Hazard	Level of risk	Precaution	Revised risk level
Ground cover	Medium	• All are made aware of uneven ground, obstructions, trip and slip risks • Site is assessed and obstructions may be removed • Routes are chosen depending on weather conditions (e.g. surface water etc)	Low
Canopy layer	Medium /High	• Staff constantly assess tree canopy for dead wood and hanging branches – these areas are segregated, or material removed when possible • Wind conditions in the canopy are monitored and locations amended dependent on weather	Low

Hazard	Level of risk	Precaution	Revised risk level
Tool use: e.g. scissors, wire cutters, knives	Medium	• Children are trained and monitored in the use of tools (safe use, safe carrying, safe cleaning and storage) • Children keep out of each other's 'blood bubble' (safe distance apart) • The appropriate tool is used for the appropriate task • Children return tools to storage location • Children sit or kneel when using tools • Tools are well maintained and in good working order • Staff monitor and manage use	Low
Handling materials: e.g. paper, art materials, sticks	Low/ Medium	• Children carry materials in an appropriate manner • Staff monitor and manage use • The appropriate material is used for the appropriate purpose	Low

Summary

It is clear when we look at the learning in this little book that it is full of potential. We can see the air around us as full of potential, from the speed that it moves, to the nature of the way that it 'plays' with leaves, sand and even our bodies. We can support children to explore the air and the way it moves through child-created wind speed indicators, or a kite that they have created themselves. As the adults, we need to explore how we can support the experimentation and failure in the learning cycle, so that learning with nature gives the child the gentle consequence of learning and therefore the attribute of perseverance. This allows the children to develop confidence as the adult supports the investigation of 20 kites that did not fly, to ultimately find the one that does. Consultation through the provocations of a Talking Tub™ and the Floorbooks™, have been shown to record children's ideas and in-depth learning that links to any outcomes from a variety of curricula across the world.

Educators and teachers around the world can hopefully see how we can teach with nature, not about nature, or even in it. This change in thinking will hopefully lead us to respect inside and outside as positive and engaging learning environments.

With kind regards

C. Warden.

Do keep in touch through **www.claire-warden.com**

or through the publishers **www.mindstretchers.com**

Mindstretchers Publications

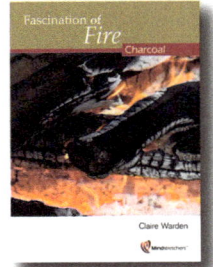

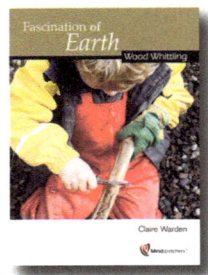

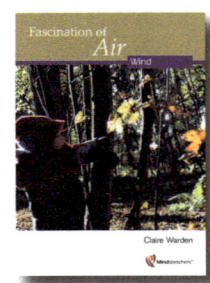

A new series of books that provide an insight into the knowledge you need as an adult to facilitate learning occurring in outdoor environments. Includes case studies with analysis and Possible Lines of Development (P.L.O.D) with full colour photography throughout.

'The true value of this little gem of a book is that it respects the power of allowing children to have their own adventures, follow their own imaginations and make their own discoveries.' Tim Gill

'An invaluable and inspirational resource, by an internationally recognized expert in her field, that beautifully illustrates the power of nature to amplify every dimension of learning.' Richard Louv

A series of 4 Fascinations: Fire; Earth; Water; Air.

E-book versions available (EPUB and Kindle)

For further details see -

www.mindstretchers.co.uk/books-and-resources/

To find out more about Claire Warden's books visit
www.claire-warden.com or go to
www.mindstretchers.com to order online.

Published by

Mindstretchers™

Email enquiries@mindstretchers.co.uk
Tel +44(0)1764 650 030

Inspirational Learning, Inside, Outside and Beyond